I0006512

NIST Special Publication 800-47

Security Guide for Interconnecting Information Technology Systems

Recommendations of the National Institute of Standards and Technology

---

COMPUTER SECURITY

Computer Security Division
Information Technology Laboratory
National Institute of Standards and Technology
Gaithersburg, MD 20899-8930

August 2002

U.S. Department of Commerce
        Donald L. Evans, Secretary

Technology Administration
        Phillip J. Bond, Under Secretary for Technology

National Institute of Standards and Technology
        Arden L. Bement, Jr., Director

Acknowledgements

The authors, Joan Hash and Tim Grance of the National Institute of Standards and Technology (NIST), and Steven Peck, Jonathan Smith, and Karen Korow-Diks of Booz Allen Hamilton, wish to thank their colleagues who reviewed drafts of this document and contributed to its technical content. We also gratefully acknowledge and appreciate the many comments we received from readers of the public and private sectors, whose valuable insights improved the quality and usefulness of this document. Finally, we wish to express thanks to the U.S. Customs Service for use of the Interconnection Security Agreement (ISA) guidance document and sample ISA, which are included in this document.

Any mention of commercial products or reference to commercial organizations is for information only; it does not imply recommendation or endorsement by NIST nor does it imply that the products mentioned are necessarily the best available for the purpose.

Table of Contents

List of Appendixes

List of Figures

EXECUTIVE SUMMARY

The *Security Guide for Interconnecting Information Technology Systems* provides guidance for planning, establishing, maintaining, and terminating interconnections between information technology (IT) systems that are owned and operated by different organizations. The guidelines are consistent with the requirements specified in the Office of Management and Budget (OMB) Circular A-130, Appendix III, for system interconnection and information sharing.

A system interconnection is defined as the direct connection of two or more IT systems for the purpose of sharing data and other information resources. The document describes various benefits of interconnecting IT systems, identifies the basic components of an interconnection, identifies methods and levels of interconnectivity, and discusses potential security risks associated with an interconnection.

The document then presents a "life-cycle management" approach for interconnecting IT systems, with an emphasis on security. The four phases of the interconnection life cycle are addressed:

+ **Planning the interconnection:** the participating organizations perform preliminary activities; examine all relevant technical, security, and administrative issues; and form an agreement governing the management, operation, and use of the interconnection.

+ **Establishing the interconnection:** the organizations develop and execute a plan for establishing the interconnection, including implementing or configuring appropriate security controls.

+ **Maintaining the interconnection:** the organizations actively maintain the interconnection after it is established to ensure that it operates properly and securely.

+ **Disconnecting the interconnection:** one or both organizations may choose to terminate the interconnection. The termination should be conducted in a planned manner to avoid disrupting the other party's system. In response to an emergency, however, one or both organizations may decide to terminate the interconnection immediately.

The document provides recommended steps for completing each phase, emphasizing security measures that should be taken to protect the connected systems and shared data.

The document also contains guides and samples for developing an Interconnection Security Agreement (ISA) and a Memorandum of Understanding/Agreement (MOU/A). The ISA specifies the technical and security requirements of the interconnection, and the MOU/A defines the responsibilities of the participating organizations. Finally, the document contains a guide for developing a System Interconnection Implementation Plan, which defines the process for establishing the interconnection, including scheduling and costs.

1. INTRODUCTION

1.1 Authority

This document has been developed by the National Institute of Standards and Technology (NIST) in furtherance of its statutory responsibilities under the Computer Security Act of 1987 and the Information Technology Management Reform Act of 1996, specifically 15 United States Code (U.S.C.) 278 g-3 (a)(5). This document is not a guideline within the meaning of 15 U.S.C 278 g-3 (a)(3).

These guidelines are for use by federal organizations that process sensitive information. They are consistent with the requirements of the Office of Management and Budget (OMB) Circular A-130, Appendix III.

This document may be used by nongovernmental organizations on a voluntary basis. It is not subject to copyright.

Nothing in this document should be taken to contradict standards and guidelines made mandatory and binding upon federal agencies by the Secretary of Commerce under statutory authority. Nor should these guidelines be interpreted as altering or superseding the existing authorities of the Secretary of Commerce, the Director of the OMB, or any other federal official.

1.2 Purpose

This document provides guidance for planning, establishing, maintaining, and terminating interconnections between information technology (IT) systems that are owned and operated by different organizations, including organizations within a single federal agency.

1.3 Scope

This document is published by the National Institute of Standards and Technology (NIST) as recommended guidance for federal agencies. It also may be used by nongovernmental (private sector) organizations. This document presents general guidelines for interconnecting IT systems. Other forms of information exchange, such as the use of browser cookies to exchange information between Web portal sites, are beyond the scope of this document, although guidance contained herein may be useful for developing such exchanges.

This document does not address classified systems or data, and it should not be used for guidance on securing such systems. Federal agencies should rely on applicable laws, regulations, and policies for interconnecting systems that are used to store, process, or transmit classified data.

1.4 Audience

This document is intended for system owners, data owners, program managers, security officers, system architects, system administrators, and network administrators who are responsible for planning, approving, establishing, maintaining, or terminating system interconnections. It is written in nontechnical language for use by a broad audience. It does not address specific information technologies.

1.5   Other Approaches to System Interconnectivity

This document provides a recommended approach for interconnecting IT systems. It is recognized, however, that many organizations have interconnected IT systems using different approaches, and some organizations follow specific procedures to meet unique operational requirements.

This document is intended only as guidance and it should not be construed as defining the only approach possible. It provides a logical framework for those organizations that have not previously interconnected IT systems, and it provides information that other organizations may use to enhance the security of existing interconnections. Organizations should tailor the guidelines to meet their specific needs and requirements.

1.6   Document Structure

This document is organized into six sections. Section 1 introduces the document. Section 2 describes the benefits of interconnecting IT systems, identifies the basic components of an interconnection, identifies methods and levels of interconnectivity, and discusses potential risks of interconnecting systems.

Sections 3 through 6 address the interconnection life-cycle. Section 3 presents recommended steps for planning a system interconnection. Section 4 provides recommended steps for establishing the interconnection. Section 5 provides recommended steps for maintaining the system interconnection after it is established. Section 6 provides guidelines for terminating the interconnection and restoring it after it is terminated.

Appendix A provides a guide for developing an Interconnection Security Agreement, which documents the technical requirements of the interconnection, as well as a sample agreement. Appendix B provides a guide for developing a Memorandum of Understanding/Agreement, which defines the responsibilities of the participating organizations, as well as a sample memorandum. Appendix C provides a guide for developing a System Interconnection Implementation Plan, which defines the process of establishing the interconnection. Appendixes D, E, and F contain a glossary, a list of references, and an index, respectively.

2.   BACKGROUND

A system interconnection is defined as the direct connection of two or more IT systems for the purpose of sharing data and other information resources. Significant benefits that can be realized through a system interconnection include: reduced operating costs, greater functionality, improved efficiency, and centralized access to data. Interconnecting IT systems may also strengthen ties among participating organizations by promoting communication and cooperation.

Organizations choose to interconnect their IT systems for a variety of reasons, depending on their organizational needs or the requirements of Executive or Congressional mandates. For example, organizations may interconnect their IT systems to—

+   Exchange data and information among selected users

+   Provide customized levels of access to proprietary databases

+   Collaborate on joint projects

+   Provide full time communications, 24 hours per day, 7 days per week

+   Provide online training

+   Provide secure storage of critical data and backup files.

A system interconnection has three basic components: two IT systems (System A and System B) and the mechanism by which they are joined (the "pipe" through which data is made available, exchanged, or passed one-way only). The components are shown in Figure 2-1. In this document, it is assumed that System A and System B are owned and operated by different organizations.

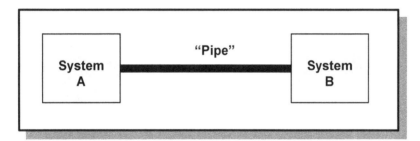

Figure 2-1. Interconnection Components

Organizations can connect their IT systems using a dedicated line that is owned by one of the organizations or is leased from a third party (e.g., an Integrated Services Digital Network [ISDN], T1, or T3 line). The private or leased line is the "pipe" that connects the IT systems. In many cases, this solution is expensive, but it can provide a high level of security for the interconnected systems, because the line may be breached only through a direct physical intrusion.

A less expensive alternative is to connect systems over a public network (e.g., the Internet), using a virtual private network (VPN). A VPN is a data network that enables two or more parties to communicate securely across a public network by creating a private connection, or "tunnel," between them. This replaces the need to rely on privately owned or leased lines. Data transmitted over a public network can be intercepted by unauthorized parties, however, necessitating the use of authentication and encryption to ensure data confidentiality and integrity. Alternately, some organizations pass data over a public network without encryption, and instead rely solely on authentication, especially if the data is publicly available or of low value. The decision to pass data over a public network should be based on an assessment of the associated risks. NIST Special Publication 800-30, *Risk Management Guide for Information Technology Systems*, provides guidance on conducting risk assessments.

There are varying levels of a system interconnection. As with any form of system access, the extent to which a party may access data and information resources is dependent on its mission and security needs. Accordingly, some organizations may choose to establish a limited interconnection, whereby users are restricted to a single application or file location, with rules governing access. Other organizations may establish a broader interconnection, enabling users to access multiple applications or databases. Still other organizations may establish an interconnection that permits full transparency and access across their respective enterprises.

Despite the advantages of an interconnection, interconnecting IT systems can expose the participating organizations to risk. If the interconnection is not properly designed, security failures could compromise the connected systems and the data that they store, process, or transmit. Similarly, if one of the connected systems is compromised, the interconnection could be used as a conduit to compromise the other system and its data. The potential for compromise is underscored by the fact that, in most cases, the participating organizations have little or no control over the operation and management of the other party's system.

It is critical, therefore, that both parties learn as much as possible about the risks associated with the planned or current interconnection and the security controls that they can implement to mitigate those risks. It also is critical that they establish an agreement between themselves regarding the management, operation, and use of the interconnection and that they formally document this agreement. The agreement should be reviewed and approved by appropriate senior staff from each organization.

Federal policy requires federal agencies to establish interconnection agreements. Specifically, OMB Circular A-130, Appendix III, requires agencies to obtain written management authorization before connecting their IT systems to other systems, based on an acceptable level of risk. The written authorization should define the rules of behavior and controls that must be maintained for the system interconnection, and it should be included in the organization's system security plan.

3. PLANNING A SYSTEM INTERCONNECTION

The process of connecting two or more IT systems should begin with a planning phase, in which the participating organizations perform preliminary activities and examine all relevant technical, security, and administrative issues. The purpose of the planning phase is to ensure that the interconnection will operate as efficiently and securely as possible. This section discusses recommended steps for planning a system interconnection, as shown in Figure 3-1.

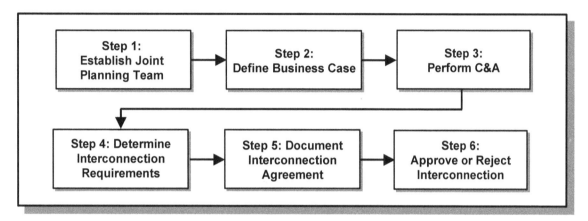

Figure 3-1. Steps to Plan a System Interconnection

3.1   Step 1: Establish a Joint Planning Team

Each organization is responsible for ensuring the security of its respective systems and data. Essential to this goal is a well-coordinated approach to interconnectivity, including regular communications between the organizations throughout the life cycle of the interconnection. Therefore, the organizations should consider establishing a joint planning team composed of appropriate managerial and technical staff, including program managers, security officers, system administrators, network administrators, and system architects.[1]

The joint planning team could be part of an existing forum or it could be created specifically for the planned interconnection. Regardless of how it is formed, the team must have the commitment and support of the system and data owners and other senior managers. The team would be responsible for coordinating all aspects of the planning process and ensuring that it had clear direction and sufficient resources. The planning team also could remain active beyond the planning phase, to serve as a forum for future discussions about issues involving the interconnection.

In addition, members of the planning team should coordinate with their colleagues who are responsible for IT capital planning, configuration management, and related activities. In most cases, the interconnection will be a component of each organization's network. By coordinating the planning of the interconnection with related activities, the organizations can reduce redundancy and promote efficiency.

3.2   Step 2: Define the Business Case

Both organizations should work together to define the purpose of the interconnection, determine how it will support their respective mission requirements, and identify potential costs and risks. Defining the

---

[1]   In some cases, the planning team could comprise a "core" of selected individuals who would consult with functional experts and specialists on an "as-needed" basis during the planning process.

business case will establish the basis of the interconnection and facilitate the planning process. Factors that should be considered are likely costs (e.g., staffing, equipment, and facilities), expected benefits (e.g., improved efficiency, centralized access to data), and potential risks (e.g., technical, legal, and financial).

As part of this process, both organizations should examine privacy issues related to data that will be exchanged or passed over the interconnection and determine whether such use is restricted under current statutes, regulations, or policies. Examples of data that might be restricted include personally identifiable information such as names and social security numbers, or confidential business information such as contractor bid rates and trade secrets. Each organization should consult with its Privacy Officer or Legal Counsel to determine whether such information may be shared or transferred. Permission to exchange or transfer data should be documented, along with a commitment to protect such data.

3.3   Step 3: Perform Certification and Accreditation

Before interconnecting their information systems, each organization should ensure that its respective system is properly certified and accredited in accordance with federal certification and accreditation (C&A) guidelines. Certification involves testing and evaluating the technical and nontechnical security features of the system to determine the extent to which it meets a set of specified security requirements. Accreditation is the official approval by a Designated Approving Authority (DAA) or other authorizing management official that the system may operate for a specific purpose using a defined set of safeguards at an acceptable level of risk.

The C&A process is applicable for both emerging systems and those already in production. It involves a series of security-related activities, including developing a system security plan, conducting a risk assessment, preparing a contingency plan, and conducting a security review. See NIST Special Publication 800-12, *An Introduction to Computer Security: The NIST Handbook*, for guidance on performing a C&A.

3.4   Step 4: Determine Interconnection Requirements

The joint planning team should identify and examine all relevant technical, security, and administrative issues surrounding the proposed interconnection. This information may be used to develop an Interconnection Security Agreement (ISA) and a Memorandum of Understanding or Agreement (MOU/A) (or an equivalent document[s]).[2] This information also may be used to develop an implementation plan for establishing the interconnection.

The joint planning team should consider the following issues:

+   *Level and Method of Interconnection:* Define the level of interconnectivity that will be established between the IT systems, ranging from limited connectivity (limited data exchange) to enterprise-level connectivity (active sharing of data and applications). In addition, describe the method used to connect the systems (dedicated line or VPN).

+   *Impact on Existing Infrastructure and Operations:* Determine whether the network or computer infrastructure currently used by both organizations is sufficient to support the interconnection, or whether additional components are required (e.g., communication lines, routers, switches, servers, and software). If additional components are required, determine the potential impact that installing and using them might have on the existing infrastructure, if any. In addition, determine the potential impact the interconnection could have on current operations, including increases in

---

[2]   Rather than develop an ISA and MOU/A, the organizations may choose to incorporate this information into a formal contract, especially if the interconnection is to be established between a federal agency and a commercial organization.

data traffic; new training requirements; and new demands on system administration, security, and maintenance.

+ *Hardware Requirements:* Identify hardware that will be needed to support the interconnection, including communications lines, routers, firewalls, hubs, switch, servers, and computer workstations. Determine whether existing hardware is sufficient, or whether additional components are required, especially if future growth is anticipated. If new hardware is required, select products that ensure interoperability.

+ *Software Requirements:* Identify software that will be needed to support the interconnection, including software for firewalls, servers, and computer workstations. Determine whether existing software is sufficient, or whether additional software is required. If new software is required, select products that ensure interoperability.

+ *Data Sensitivity:* Identify the sensitivity level of data or information resources that will be made available, exchanged, or passed one-way only across the interconnection. Identifying data sensitivity is critical for determining the security controls that should be used to protect the connected systems and data. Examples of sensitive data include financial data, personal information, and proprietary business data. See NIST Special Publication 800-18, *Guide for Developing Security Plans for Information Technology Systems*, for further guidance.

+ *User Community:* Define the community of users who will access, exchange, or receive data across the interconnection. Determine whether users must possess certain characteristics corresponding to data sensitivity levels, such as employment status or nationality requirements, and whether background checks and security clearances are required.[3] Devise an approach for compiling and managing the profiles of all users who will have access to the interconnection, including user identification, workstation addresses, workstation type, operating system, and any other relevant information. Each organization should use this information to develop and maintain a comprehensive database of its users.

+ *Services and Applications:* Identify the information services that will be provided over the interconnection by each organization and the applications associated with those services, if appropriate. Examples of services include e-mail, file transfer protocol (FTP), RADIUS, Kerberos, database query, file query, and general computational services.

+ *Security Controls:* Identify security controls that will be implemented to protect the confidentiality, integrity, and availability of the connected systems and the data that will pass between them. Controls can be selected from the examples provided in Section 4 or from other sources. Controls should be appropriate for the systems that will be connected and the environment in which the interconnection will operate.

+ *Segregation of Duties:* Determine whether the management or execution of certain duties should be divided between two or more individuals. Examples of duties that might be segregated include auditing, managing user profiles, and maintaining equipment. Segregation of duties reduces the risk that a single individual could cause harm to the connected systems and data, either accidentally or deliberately.

+ *Incident Reporting and Response:* Establish procedures to report and respond to anomalous and suspicious activity that is detected by either technology or staff. Determine when and how to

---

[3] If an interconnection is to be established between agencies representing different levels of government (e.g., federal and state, federal and local), each party should be cognizant of the other's rules governing background checks and security clearances.

notify each other about security incidents that could affect the interconnection. Identify the types of information that will be reported, including the cause of the incident, affected data or programs, and actual or potential impact. In addition, identify types of incidents that require a coordinated response, and determine how to coordinate response activities. It might be appropriate to develop a joint incident response plan for this purpose. For more information, see NIST Special Publication 800-3, *Establishing a Computer Security Incidence Response Capability (CSIRC)*, and Federal Computer Incident Response Center (FedCIRC) publications.

+ *Contingency Planning:* Each organization should have a contingency plan(s) to respond to and recover from disasters and other disruptive contingencies that could affect its IT system, ranging from the failure of system components to the loss of computing facilities. Determine how to notify each other of such contingencies, the extent to which the organizations will assist each other, and the terms under which assistance will be provided. Identify emergency points of contact (POC). Determine whether to incorporate redundancy into components supporting the interconnection, including redundant interconnection points, and how to retrieve data backups. Coordinate disaster response training, testing, and exercises. See NIST Special Publication 800-34, *Contingency Planning Guide for Information Technology Systems*, for more information.

+ *Data Element Naming and Ownership:* Determine whether the data element naming schemes used by both organizations are compatible, or whether new databases must be normalized so the organizations can use data passed over the interconnection. In addition, determine whether ownership of data is transferred from the transmitting party to the receiving party, or whether the transmitting party retains ownership and the receiver becomes the custodian. As part of this effort, determine how transferred data will be stored, whether data may be re-used, and how data will be destroyed. In addition, determine how to identify and resolve potential data element naming conflicts.

+ *Data Backup:* Determine whether data or information that is passed across the interconnection must be backed up and stored. If backups are required, identify the types of data that will be backed up, how frequently backups will be conducted (daily, weekly, or monthly), and whether backups will be performed by one or both parties. Also, determine how to perform backups, and how to link backups to contingency plan procedures. Critical data should be backed up regularly, stored in a secure off-site location to prevent loss or damage, and retained for a period approved by both parties. Similarly, audit logs should be copied, stored in a secure location, and retained for a period approved by both parties.

+ *Change Management:* Determine how to coordinate the planning, design, and implementation of changes that could affect the connected systems or data, such as upgrading hardware or software, or adding services. Establish a forum with appropriate staff from each organization to review proposed changes to the interconnection, as appropriate. Coordinating change management activities will reduce the potential for implementing changes that could disrupt the availability or integrity of data, or introduce vulnerabilities.

+ *Rules of Behavior:* Develop rules of behavior that clearly delineate the responsibilities and expected behavior of all personnel who will be authorized to access the interconnection. The rules should be in writing, and they should state the consequences of inconsistent behavior or noncompliance. The rules should be covered in a security training and awareness program.

+ *Security Training and Awareness:* Define a security training and awareness program for all authorized personnel who will be involved in managing, using, and/or operating the interconnection. The program may be incorporated into current security training and awareness activities. Identify training requirements, including frequency and scheduling, and assign responsibility for conducting training and awareness activities. Design training to ensure that personnel are familiar with IT security policy, procedures, and the rules of behavior associated with the interconnection. Require users to sign an acknowledgement form indicating that they understand their security responsibilities, if appropriate. If shared applications are used, ensure users know how to use them properly. If the interconnection is used to exchange or transfer sensitive data, ensure that users understand special requirements for handling such data, if required. See NIST Special Publication 800-50, *Building an Information Technology Security Awareness and Training Program,* for guidance.

+ *Roles and Responsibilities:* Identify personnel who will be responsible for establishing, maintaining, or managing the interconnection, including managers, system administrators, application designers, auditors, security staff, and specialists from such fields as insurance and risk management. Choose personnel who have appropriate subject matter expertise. If contractors are involved, one or both organizations may be required to develop a nondisclosure agreement to safeguard the confidentiality and integrity of exchanged data.

+ *Scheduling:* Develop a preliminary schedule for all activities involved in planning, establishing, and maintaining the interconnection. Also, determine the schedule and conditions for terminating or reauthorizing the interconnection. For example, both parties might agree to review the interconnection every 12 months to determine whether to reauthorize it for continued operation.

+ *Costs and Budgeting:* Identify the expected costs required to plan, establish, and maintain the interconnection. Identify all associated costs, including labor, hardware, software, communications lines, applications, facilities, physical security, training, and testing. Also, identify costs for certifying and accrediting the interconnection after it is established, if appropriate. Develop a comprehensive budget, and determine how costs will be apportioned between the parties, if required.

3.5 Step 5: Document Interconnection Agreement

The joint planning team should document an agreement governing the interconnection and the terms under which the organizations will abide by the agreement, based on the team's review of all relevant technical, security, and administrative issues (Section 3.4 above). Two documents may be developed: an ISA and an MOU/A. These documents are discussed below.[4]

Because the ISA and the MOU/A may contain sensitive information, they should be stored in a secure location to protect against theft, damage, or destruction. If copies are stored electronically, they should be protected from unauthorized disclosure or modification. An ISA development guide and sample are provided in Appendix A, and an MOU/A development guide and sample are provided in Appendix B.

3.5.1 Substep 1: Develop an Interconnection Security Agreement

The ISA is a security document that specifies the technical and security requirements for establishing, operating, and maintaining the interconnection. It also supports the MOU/A between the organizations. Specifically, the ISA documents the requirements for connecting the IT systems, describes the security controls that will be used to protect the systems and data, contains a topological drawing of the interconnection, and provides a signature line.

---

[4]   In some cases, the organizations may decide to use established organizational procedures for documenting the agreement, in lieu of an ISA and MOU/A.

3.5.2 Substep 2: Establish a Memorandum of Understanding (or Agreement)

The MOU/A documents the terms and conditions for sharing data and information resources in a secure manner. Specifically, the MOU/A defines the purpose of the interconnection; identifies relevant authorities; specifies the responsibilities of both organizations; and defines the terms of agreement, including apportionment of costs and the timeline for terminating or reauthorizing the interconnection. The MOU/A should not include technical details on how the interconnection is established or maintained; that is the function of the ISA.

3.6 Step 6: Approve or Reject System Interconnection

The joint planning team should submit the ISA and the MOU/A to the DAA or other authorizing management official of each organization, requesting approval for the interconnection. Upon receipt, the DAAs should review the ISA, the MOU/A, and any other relevant documentation or activities, including those addressed in Section 4. Based on this review, the DAAs should decide on one of the following:

+ Approve the interconnection

+ Grant interim approval

+ Reject the interconnection.

If the DAAs (or other authorizing officials) accept the ISA and the MOU/A, they should sign and date the documents, thereby approving the interconnection. The documents should then be given to an appropriate security officer from each organization to retain. A signed copy of the documents also should be forwarded to the appropriate program manager or any other officials responsible for interconnections within each organization.

One or both DAAs may decide to grant an interim approval. Interim approval may be granted if the planned interconnection does not meet the requirements stated in the ISA, but mission criticality requires that the interconnection must be established and cannot be delayed. The DAA(s) should provide a signed letter to the respective security officers and to the other DAA, specifying the tasks that must be completed before full approval will be granted, including the implementation of additional security controls, if required. In addition, the DAA(s) should specify timelines for completing the tasks, although ideally the tasks should be completed before the interconnection is operational. The joint planning team should then work to meet the requirements specified by the DAA(s).

If one or both DAAs reject the interconnection, the joint planning team should return to the planning process. In this situation, the DAA(s) should provide a signed letter to the respective program managers and to the other DAA, specifying the reason(s) for rejecting the planned interconnection and proposing solutions. The DAA(s) also should meet with the joint planning team to discuss and agree on the proposed solutions and timelines for correcting specified deficiencies, so approval may be granted.

4.   ESTABLISHING A SYSTEM INTERCONNECTION

After the system interconnection is planned and approved, it may be implemented. This section provides recommended steps for establishing the system interconnection, as shown in Figure 4-1.

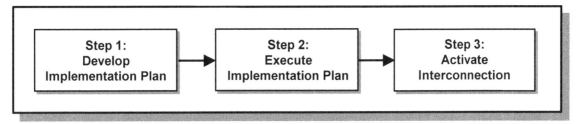

Figure 4-1. Steps to Establish a System Interconnection

4.1   Step 1: Develop an Implementation Plan

To ensure that the IT systems are connected properly and securely, the joint planning team should develop a System Interconnection Implementation Plan. The purpose of the plan is to centralize all aspects of the interconnection effort in one document and to clarify how technical requirements specified in the ISA will be implemented. A well-developed implementation plan will greatly improve the likelihood that the interconnection will operate successfully and securely.

At a minimum, the implementation plan should—

+   Describe the IT systems that will be connected

+   Identify the sensitivity or classification level of data that will be made available, exchanged, or passed one-way across the interconnection

+   Identify personnel who will establish and maintain the interconnection, and specify their responsibilities

+   Identify implementation tasks and procedures

+   Identify and describe security controls that will be used to protect the confidentiality, integrity, and availability of the connected systems and data (see Section 4.2.1 for sample security controls).

+   Provide test procedures and measurement criteria to ensure that the interconnection operates properly and securely

+   Specify training requirements for users, including a training schedule

+   Cite or include all relevant documentation, such as system security plans, design specifications, and standard operating procedures.

A guide for developing a System Interconnection Implementation Plan is provided in Appendix C.

4.2   Step 2: Execute the Implementation Plan

After the implementation plan is developed, it should be reviewed and approved by senior members of the planning team. Pending approval, it may then be executed. A list of recommended tasks for establishing an interconnection is provided below. Detailed procedures associated with each task should be described in the implementation plan.

4.2.1   Substep 1: Implement or Configure Security Controls

If security controls are not in place or they are configured improperly, the process of establishing the interconnection could expose the IT systems to access by unauthorized personnel. Therefore, the first step is to implement appropriate security controls or to configure existing controls, as specified in the ISA and the implementation plan. Security controls may include the following:

+   *Firewalls:* Firewalls determine whether data packets are permitted into a network, and they restrict access to specific resources. Install firewalls to protect internal networks and other resources from unauthorized access across the interconnection, or configure existing firewalls accordingly. If the interconnection involves the use of servers, host them in a separately protected "demilitarized zone" (DMZ), which may be accomplished by installing two firewalls: one on the external line and one at the connection to internal networks. (Alternately, a firewall could be installed on the external line and a security portal installed at the internal connection.) Ensure firewall ports are configured properly and change all default passwords. See NIST Special Publication 800-41, *Guidelines on Firewalls and Firewall Policy*, for more information.

+   *Intrusion Detection:* An intrusion detection system (IDS) detects security breaches by looking for anomalies in normal activities, by looking for patterns of activity that are associated with intrusions or insider misuse, or both. One or both organizations should implement an IDS (or configure existing IDSs) to detect undesirable or malicious activity that could affect the interconnection or data that pass over it. A combination of network-based and host-based IDSs may be used, if appropriate. Configure alert mechanisms to notify system administrators or security officers when intrusions or unusual activities are detected. See NIST Special Publication 800-31, *Intrusion Detection Systems (IDS)*, for more information.

+   *Auditing:* Install or configure mechanisms to record activities occurring across the interconnection, including application processes and user activities. Activities that should be recorded include event type, date and time of event, user identification, workstation identification, the success or failure of access attempts, and security actions taken by system administrators or security officers. Audit logs should have read-only access, and only authorized personnel should have access to the logs. In addition, logs should be stored in a secure location to protect against theft and damage, and they should be retained for a period approved by both parties.

+   *Identification and Authentication:* Identification and authentication is used to prevent unauthorized personnel from entering an IT system. Implement strong mechanisms to identify and authenticate users to ensure that they are authorized to access the interconnection. Mechanisms that may be used include user identification and passwords, digital certificates, authentication tokens, biometrics, and smart cards.

    If passwords are used, they should be at least eight characters long, have a mixture of alphabetic and numeric characters, and be changed at predetermined intervals. Master password files should be encrypted and protected from unauthorized access. If digital signatures are used, the technology must conform to Federal Information Processing Standard (FIPS) 186-2, *Digital Signature Standard (DSS)*.[5]

    Depending on data sensitivity, organizations may permit users to access the interconnection after

---

[5]   This requirement applies only to federal agencies.

they have authenticated to their local domain, reducing the need for multiple passwords or other mechanisms. Applications operating across the interconnection could rely on authentication information from the user's local domain, using a proxy authentication mechanism.

+ *Logical Access Controls:* Logical access controls are mechanisms used to designate users who have access to system resources and the types of transactions and functions they are permitted to perform. Use access control lists (ACL) and access rules to specify the access privileges of authorized personnel, including the level of access and the types of transactions and functions that are permitted (e.g., read, write, execute, delete, create, and search). Hardware and software often are configured with ACLs, or the ACLs may be administered offline and then distributed to routers and other devices. Configure access rules to grant appropriate access privileges to authorized personnel, based on their roles or job functions. Ensure only system administrators have access to the controls.

  In addition, install a log-on warning banner notifying unauthorized users that they have accessed a federal computer system and unauthorized use can be punishable by fines or imprisonment. Ensure that the terms of the warning have been approved by each organization's Legal Counsel. A user's acceptance of the warning should constitute consent to monitoring. See NIST Special Publication 800-18, *Guide for Developing Security Plans for Information Technology Systems*, for more information on warning banners.

+ *Virus Scanning:* Data and information that pass from one IT system to the other should be scanned with antivirus software to detect and eliminate malicious code, including viruses, worms, and Trojan horses. Install antivirus software on all servers and computer workstations linked to the interconnection. Ensure the software is automatically updated and properly maintained with current virus definitions. In addition, incorporate virus scanning into user training to ensure that users understand how to scan computers, file downloads, and e-mail attachments, if appropriate. Develop procedures and assign responsibilities for responding to and recovering from malicious code attacks.

+ *Encryption:* Encryption is used to ensure that data cannot be read or modified by unauthorized users. When used properly, encryption will protect the confidentiality and integrity of data during transmission and storage, and it may be used for authentication and nonrepudiation. Encryption may be implemented in devices such as routers, switches, firewalls, servers, and computer workstations. Configure devices to apply the appropriate level of encryption required for data that pass over the interconnection. If required, implement encryption mechanisms (e.g., digital signatures) to authenticate users to the interconnection and to shared applications, and to provide nonrepudiation. Federal agencies must use FIPS-approved algorithms and cryptographic modules if they use cryptographic methods.

+ *Physical and Environmental Security:* Physical security addresses the physical protection of computer hardware and software. Place hardware and software supporting the interconnection, including interconnection points, in a secure location that is protected from unauthorized access, interference, or damage. Ensure that environmental controls are in place to protect against hazards such as fire, water, and excessive heat and humidity. In addition, place computer workstations in secure areas to protect them from damage, loss, theft, or unauthorized physical access. Consider using access badges, cipher locks, or biometric devices to control access to secure areas. Also, consider using biometric devices to prevent unauthorized use of workstations. For guidance, see the following NIST Special Publications: 800-12, *An Introduction to Computer Security: The NIST Handbook*, 800-30, *Risk Management Guide for Information Technology Systems*, and 800-27, *Engineering Principles for Information Technology Security (A Baseline for Achieving Security)*.

4.2.2   Substep 2: Install or Configure Hardware and Software

After security controls are installed or configured, it may be necessary to install new hardware and software to establish the interconnection, or to configure existing hardware and software for this purpose, if appropriate. Place hardware and software in secure areas that are configured with proper environmental controls. The following equipment might be required:

+ *Communications Line:* If a dedicated line is used for the interconnection, ensure that the line is connected to the appropriate physical site at each organization.

+ *VPN:* Install VPN software on servers and local workstations, and configure it appropriately.

+ *Routers and Switches:* Install routers or switches to connect to the communications line between the IT systems, or configure existing devices.

+ *Hubs:* Install hubs to join multiple computers into a single network segment, if required.

+ *Servers:* Install appropriate servers to support services provided across the interconnection, such as database, Web, and application servers. If existing servers are used, determine whether the hardware should be upgraded to support the interconnection, and whether the latest software and security patches have been applied.

+ *Computer Workstations:* Configure computer workstations by providing a menu option or a link to enable authorized users to invoke the interconnection. Install appropriate client software, if required.

4.2.3   Substep 3: Integrate Applications

Integrate applications or protocols for services that are provided across the interconnection. Examples include word processing, database applications, e-mail, Web browsers, application servers, authentication servers, domain servers, development tools, editing programs, and communications programs. If using Web-based applications, consider the possible security ramifications of integrating the use of Java, JavaScript, ActiveX, and cookies. See the following NIST Special Publications for more information: 800-27, *Engineering Principles for Information Technology Security (A Baseline for Achieving Security),* 800-28, *Guidelines on Active Content and Mobile Code,* and 800-33, *Underlying Technical Models for Information Technology Security.*

4.2.4   Substep 4: Conduct Operational and Security Testing

Conduct a series of tests to ensure equipment operates properly and there are no obvious ways for unauthorized users to circumvent or defeat security controls.[6] Test the interface between applications across the interconnection, and simulate data traffic at planned activity levels to verify correct translation at the receiving end(s). Test security controls under realistic conditions. If possible, conduct testing in an isolated, nonoperational environment to avoid affecting the IT systems.

Document the results of the testing and compare them with a set of predetermined operational and security standards approved by both organizations. Determine whether the results meet a mutually agreed level of acceptable risk and whether other actions are required. Correct weaknesses or problems and document the actions taken. Retest the interconnection to ensure that weaknesses or problems are eliminated and that new flaws have not been introduced.

---

[6]   Operational and security testing may be performed as part of recertification and reaccreditation discussed in Section 4.2.7.

4.2.5 Substep 5: Conduct Security Training and Awareness

Conduct security training and awareness for all authorized personnel who will be involved in managing, using, and/or operating the interconnection. Provide training and awareness for new users and refresher training for all users periodically. Distribute the rules of behavior to all personnel who will be authorized to access the interconnection. Require them to sign an acknowledgement form confirming that they understand the rules before granting them authorization to access the interconnection, according to organizational policy. In addition, ensure that the staff know how to report suspicious or prohibited activity, and how to request assistance if they encounter problems.

4.2.6 Substep 6: Update System Security Plans

Both organizations should update their system security plans and related documents to reflect the changed security environment in which their respective system operates. In addition, consider conducting mutual reviews of those sections of the updated plans that are relevant to the interconnection. The details for conducting a mutual review should be addressed in the MOU/A.

It is recommended the security plans include the following information regarding the system interconnection (and other interconnections, if appropriate):

+ Names of interconnected systems

+ Organization owning the other systems

+ Type of interconnection

+ Short discussion of major concerns or considerations in determining interconnection

+ Name and title of authorizing management official(s)

+ Date of authorization

+ System of record, if applicable (Privacy Act data)

+ Sensitivity level of each system

+ Interaction among systems

+ Hardware inventory

+ Software inventory

+ Security concerns and rules of behavior governing the interconnection.

See NIST Special Publication 800-18, *Guide for Developing Security Plans for Information Technology Systems*, for more information.

4.2.7 Substep 7: Perform Recertification and Reaccreditation

Establishing an interconnection may represent a significant change to the connected systems. Before proceeding further, each organization should consider recertifying and reaccrediting its respective system to verify that security protection remains acceptable. Recertification and reaccreditation involve the same activities described in Section 3.3. A full C&A might not be necessary, however, if the system continues to operate within an acceptable level of risk; instead, an abbreviated C&A might be sufficient. See NIST Special Publications 800-12, *An Introduction to Computer Security: The NIST Handbook*, for guidance.

4.3   Step 3: Activate the Interconnection

Activate the interconnection for use by both parties, following prescribed guidelines. It is recommended that one or both organizations closely monitor the interconnection for a period of at least three months to ensure that it operates properly and securely. Analyze audit logs carefully and frequently, and monitor the types of assistance requested by users. Document any weaknesses or problems that occur and correct them.

5. MAINTAINING A SYSTEM INTERCONNECTION

After the interconnection is established, it must be actively maintained to ensure that it operates properly and securely. This section describes the following recommended activities for maintaining the interconnection:

+ Maintain clear lines of communication

+ Maintain equipment

+ Manage user profiles

+ Conduct security reviews

+ Analyze audit logs

+ Report and respond to security incidents

+ Coordinate contingency planning activities

+ Perform change management

+ Maintain system security plans.

5.1 Maintain Clear Lines of Communication

It is critical that both organizations maintain clear lines of communication and communicate regularly. Open lines of communication help to ensure that the interconnection is properly maintained and that security controls remain effective. Open communications also facilitate change management activities by making it easy for both sides to notify each other about planned system changes that could affect the interconnection. Finally, maintaining clear lines of communication enables both sides to promptly notify each other of security incidents and system disruptions and helps them to conduct coordinated responses, if necessary.

Communications should be conducted between designated personnel using approved procedures, as specified in the ISA. Information that should be shared includes the following:

+ Initial agreements and changes to agreements

+ Changes in designated management and technical personnel

+ Activities related to establishing and maintaining the interconnection

+ Change management activities that could affect the interconnection

+ Security incidents that could affect the connected systems and data

+ Disasters and other contingencies that disrupt one or both of the connected systems

+ Termination of the interconnection

+ Planned restoration of the interconnection.

Information may be exchanged verbally or in writing, depending on the nature of the communications. However, any activities that could change, modify, or adjust one or both of the connected systems should always be communicated in writing.

5.2 Maintain Equipment

The organizations should agree on who will maintain the equipment used to operate the interconnection, to ensure its continued integrity and availability. Equipment should be maintained at regular service intervals and in accordance with manufacturer specifications. Only authorized personnel should be allowed to service and repair equipment, according to established organizational policy. All maintenance activities and corrective actions should be documented, and the records should be stored in a secure location. Finally, organizations should notify each other before performing maintenance activities, including scheduled outages.

5.3 Manage User Profiles

Both organizations should actively manage user profiles. If a user resigns or changes job responsibilities, the appropriate organization should update the user's profile to prevent access to data or information that is no longer appropriate. Establish procedures for investigating, disabling, and terminating access to users who do not actively access the interconnection over a specific period of time. For example, access privileges for users who do not access the interconnection after a predetermined number of days should be disabled, pending confirmation that they still require access. Privileges for users who do not access the interconnection after a (longer) predetermined period should be terminated. Such measures help prevent intruders from exploiting inactive accounts to masquerade as legitimate users.

5.4 Conduct Security Reviews

One or both organizations should review the security controls for the interconnection at least annually or whenever a significant change occurs to ensure they are operating properly and are providing appropriate levels of protection. A variety of security assessment tools are available commercially that can be run against firewalls and other controls to identify administrative and configuration vulnerabilities and other security risks. Penetration tests also should be conducted. See NIST Special Publication 800-42, *Guidelines on Network Security Testing*, for a methodology for using network-based tools to test IT systems for vulnerabilities.

Security reviews may be conducted by designated audit authorities of one or both organizations, or by an independent third party. Both organizations should agree on the rigor and frequency of reviews as well as a reporting process. For example, both organizations should examine the results of security reviews to identify areas requiring attention. Security risks or problems should be corrected or addressed in a timely manner. Corrective actions should be documented, and the records should be stored in a secure location.

5.5 Analyze Audit Logs

One or both organizations should analyze audit logs at predetermined intervals to detect and track unusual or suspicious activities across the interconnection that might indicate intrusions or internal misuse. Given the voluminous nature of audit logs, the logs should be kept at a manageable size by setting logging levels appropriately. Automated tools should be used to scan for anomalies, unusual patterns, and known attack signatures, and to alert a system administrator if a threat is detected. In addition, an experienced system administrator (or more than one, if segregation of duties is applied) should periodically review the logs to detect patterns of suspicious activity that scanning tools might not recognize. Audit logs should be retained for a period approved by both parties.

5.6   Report and Respond to Security Incidents

Both organizations should notify each other of intrusions, attacks, or internal misuse, so the other party can take steps to determine whether its system has been compromised. Both organizations should take appropriate steps to isolate and respond to such incidents, in accordance with their respective incident response procedures. Actions that may be taken include shutting down a computer, disabling an account, reconfiguring a router or firewall, or shutting down the system. If the incident involves personnel from one or both organizations, disciplinary actions may be required.

In some cases, both parties should coordinate their incident response activities, especially if a major security breach occurs. If the incident was an attack or an intrusion attempt, appropriate law enforcement authorities should be notified, and all attempts should be made to preserve evidence. All security incidents, along with the reporting and response actions taken, should be documented. See NIST Special Publication 800-3, *Establishing a Computer Security Incidence Response Capability (CSIRC)*, and FedCIRC publications for more information.

5.7   Coordinate Contingency Planning Activities

Both organizations should coordinate contingency planning training, testing, and exercises to minimize the impact of disasters and other contingencies that could damage the connected systems or jeopardize the confidentiality and integrity of shared data. Special attention should be given to emergency alert and notification; damage assessment; and response and recovery, including data retrieval. The organizations should consider developing joint procedures based on existing contingency plans, if appropriate. Finally, the organizations should notify each other about changes to emergency POC information (primary and alternate), including changes in staffing, addresses, telephone and fax numbers, and e-mail addresses. See NIST Special Publication 800-34, *Contingency Planning Guide for Information Technology Systems*, for more information.

5.8   Perform Change Management

Effective change management is critical to ensure the interconnection is properly maintained and secured. Each organization should establish a change control board (CCB), or a similar body, to review and approve planned changes to its respective system, such as upgrading software or adding services.

The decision to upgrade or modify a system should be based on the security requirements specified in the ISA and a determination that the change will not adversely affect the interconnection. Accordingly, planned changes should be tested in an isolated, nonoperational environment to avoid affecting the IT systems, if possible. In addition, the other party should be notified in writing of the changes, and it should be involved in this process. After approving a change, the CCB would be responsible for managing and tracking the change to ensure it did not harm the interconnection, either by disrupting service or by introducing vulnerabilities.

If a planned change is designed specifically for the interconnection, both parties should establish a joint CCB or a similar body to review and approve the change. In most cases, such changes are designed to improve the operation and security of the interconnection, such as by adding new functions, improving user interfaces, and eliminating (or mitigating) known vulnerabilities. Nevertheless, it is critical that both organizations carefully review such changes before implementing them and that they manage and track the changes after they are made. Any vulnerabilities or problems should be corrected in a timely manner.

5.9   Maintain System Security Plans

Both organizations should update their system security plans and other relevant documentation at least annually or whenever there is a significant change to their IT systems or to the interconnection. Refer to NIST Special Publication 800-18, *Guide for Developing Security Plans for Information Technology Systems*, for information on updating system security plans.

6. DISCONNECTING A SYSTEM INTERCONNECTION

This section describes the process for terminating the system interconnection. If possible, the interconnection should be terminated in a methodical manner to avoid disrupting the other party's IT system.

6.1 Planned Disconnection

The decision to terminate the interconnection should be made by the system owner with the advice of appropriate managerial and technical staff. Before terminating the interconnection, the initiating party should notify the other party in writing, and it should receive an acknowledgment in return. The notification should describe the reason(s) for the disconnection, provide the proposed timeline for the disconnection, and identify technical and management staff who will conduct the disconnection.

An organization might have a variety of reasons to terminate an interconnection, including:

+ Changed business needs

+ Failed security audits, including increases in risks that rise to unacceptable levels

+ Inability to abide by the technical specifications of the ISA

+ Inability to abide by the terms and conditions of the MOU/A

+ Cost considerations, including increases in the cost of maintaining the interconnection

+ Changes in system configuration or in the physical location of equipment.

The schedule for terminating the interconnection should permit a reasonable period for internal business planning so both sides can make appropriate preparations, including notifying affected users and identifying alternative resources for continuing operations. In addition, managerial and technical staff from both organizations should coordinate to determine the logistics of the disconnection and the disposition of shared data, including purging and overwriting sensitive data (data remanence). The disconnection should be conducted when the impact on users is minimal, based on known activity patterns. Following the disconnection, each organization should update its system security plan and related documents to reflect the changed security environment in which its respective system operates.

6.2 Emergency Disconnection

If one or both organizations detect an attack, intrusion attempt, or other contingency that exploits or jeopardizes the connected systems or their data, it might be necessary to abruptly terminate the interconnection without providing written notice to the other party. This extraordinary measure should be taken only in extreme circumstances and only after consultation with appropriate technical staff and senior management.[7]

The decision to make an emergency disconnection should be made by the system owner and implemented by technical staff. If the system owner is unavailable, a predesignated staff member may authorize the disconnection in accordance with written criteria that stipulate the conditions under which this authority is exercised.

---

[7] Each organization should consult with its Legal Counsel well in advance of a potential emergency disconnection to address issues related to liability, investigation, and evidence preservation.

The system owner or designee should immediately notify the other party's emergency contact by telephone or other verbal method, and receive confirmation of the notification. Both parties should work together to isolate and investigate the incident, including conducting a damage assessment and reviewing audit logs and security controls, in accordance with incident response procedures. If the incident was an attack or an intrusion attempt, law enforcement authorities should be notified, and all attempts should be made to preserve evidence.

The initiating party should provide a written notification to the other party in a timely manner (e.g., within five days). The notification should describe the nature of the incident, explain why the interconnection was terminated, describe how the interconnection was terminated, and identify actions taken to isolate and investigate the incident. In addition, the notification may specify when and under what conditions the interconnection may be restored, if appropriate.

6.3 Restoration of Interconnection

Both organizations may choose to restore the system interconnection after it has been terminated. The decision to restore the interconnection should be based on the cause and duration of the disconnection. For example, if the interconnection was terminated because of an attack, intrusion, or other contingency, both parties should implement appropriate countermeasures to prevent a recurrence of the problem. They also should modify the ISA and MOU/A to address issues requiring attention, if necessary. Alternately, if the interconnection has been terminated for more than 90 days, each party should perform a risk assessment on its respective system, and reexamine all relevant planning and implementation issues, including developing a new ISA and MOU/A.

Appendix A—Interconnection Security Agreement

The organizations that own and operate the connected information technology (IT) systems should develop an Interconnection Security Agreement (ISA) (or an equivalent document) to document the technical requirements of the interconnection. The ISA also supports a Memorandum of Understanding or Agreement (MOU/A) between the organizations (see Appendix B). An ISA development guide is provided below; a sample ISA is depicted in Figure A-1 at the end of this appendix.

A.1   Purpose

The intent of the ISA is to document and formalize the interconnection arrangements between "Organization A" and "Organization B" and to specify any details that may be required to provide overall security safeguards for the systems being interconnected. General guidance regarding the contents of an ISA is provided below; however, an ISA may be tailored by mutual consent of the participating organizations. A system that is approved by an ISA for interconnection with one organization's system should meet the protection requirements equal to, or greater than, those implemented by the other organization's system.

A.2   References

The authority for interconnectivity between IT systems is based on Office of Management and Budget (OMB) Circular A-130 and a signed MOU/A between the two organizations that are establishing the interconnection.

A.3   Scope

This procedure is effective in the following System Development Life Cycle (SDLC) phases:

CONCEPTS DEVELOPMENT		DEPLOYMENT	√
DESIGN		OPERATIONS	√
DEVELOPMENT	√	DISPOSAL	√

A.4   Procedure

An ISA is used to support an MOU/A that establishes the requirements for data exchange between two organizations. The MOU/A is used to document the business and legal requirements necessary to support the business relations between the two organizations. The MOU/A should not include technical details regarding how the interconnection is established; that is the function of the ISA. An ISA is a distinct security-related document that outlines the technical solution and security requirements for the interconnection. It does not replace an MOU/A. As older MOU/As are updated, they should be changed to refer to the appropriate ISA covering the connectivity addressed by the MOU/A.

An ISA can be signed only by the two Designated Approval Authorities (DAA) (or other authorizing management officials) whose names appear in Section 4 of the agreement (see below). *The ISA should be formally signed before the interconnection is declared operational.*

A.5   Contents of an Interconnection Security Agreement

An ISA should contain a cover sheet followed by a document of four numbered sections. The information presented within those four sections should address the need for the interconnection and the security controls required and implemented to protect the confidentiality, integrity, and availability of the systems and data. The extent of the information should be sufficient for the two DAAs to make a prudent decision about approving the interconnection. The four sections are as follows:

+   Section 1: Interconnection Statement of Requirements

+   Section 2: Systems Security Considerations

+   Section 3: Topological Drawing

+   Section 4: Signatory Authority.

It is difficult to define the required security considerations that may need to be documented without having detailed knowledge of each system being connected. The items in Section 2 should be included by mutual consent. Therefore, a technical representative from each organization who understands that organization's system should choose which security issues are relevant in Section 2. One system may have several security requirements that must be documented and that may not apply to the other system. The technical representative for each organization should have the authority to represent his or her DAA for defining requirements for the particular ISA.

A.6   Section 1: Interconnection Statement of Requirements

Use this section to document the formal requirement for connecting the two systems. Explain the rationale for the interconnection to the two DAAs. Enter a one- or two-paragraph statement justifying the interconnection. Within the information presented, include the following information:

+   The requirement for the interconnection, including the benefits derived.

+   The names of the systems being interconnected.

+   The agency name or organization that initiated the requirement. If the requirement is generated by a higher level agency or organization, indicate the name of the organization and the individual, if appropriate, that requested the interconnection.

A.7   Section 2: System Security Considerations

Use this section to document the security features that are in place to protect the confidentiality, integrity, and availability of the data and the systems being interconnected. The technical representative from each organization should discuss the contents on this section to come to a mutual agreement as to which items will be included. Both organizations should answer each item, even if only one party is affected by the item in question. Note that some items are recommended, whereas others are optional. Optional items affecting only one system should be answered and included.

SUGGESTED ITEMS: *(Do not include the title "Suggested Items" in the ISA.) The following items should be addressed in the ISA:*

+   *General Information/Data Description.* Describe the information and data that will be made available, exchanged, or passed one-way only by the interconnection of the two systems.

+ *Services Offered.* Describe the nature of the information services (e.g., e-mail, file transfer protocol [FTP], database query, file query, general computational services) offered over the interconnection by each organization.

+ *Data Sensitivity.* Enter the sensitivity level of the information that will be handled through the interconnection, including the highest level of sensitivity involved (e.g., Privacy Act, Trade Secret Act, Law Enforcement Sensitive, Sensitive-But-Unclassified) and the most restrictive protection measures required.

+ *User Community.* Describe the "user community" that will be served by the interconnection, including their approved access levels and the lowest approval level of any individual who will have access to the interconnection. Also, discuss requirements for background investigations and security clearances, if appropriate.

+ *Information Exchange Security.* Describe all system security technical services pertinent to the secure exchange of data between the connected systems.

+ *Rules of Behavior.* Summarize the aspects of behavior expected from users who will have access to the interconnection. Each system is expected to protect information belonging to the other through the implementation of security controls that protect against intrusion, tampering, and viruses, among others. Do not enter statements of law or policy. Such statements typically are addressed in the MOU/A.

+ *Formal Security Policy.* Enter the titles of the formal security policy(ies) that govern each system (e.g., "Information Systems Policy and Procedures, Number xxxx" for "Organization A").

+ *Incident Reporting.* Describe the agreements made regarding the reporting of and response to information security incidents for both organizations. For example, "Each organization will report incidents in accordance to its own (procedure name) procedures." If no incident reporting is performed, so state.

+ *Audit Trail Responsibilities.* Describe how the audit trail responsibility will be shared by the organizations and what events each organization will log. Specify the length of time that audit logs will be retained. If no audit trail is performed, so state.

OTHER ITEMS:[8] *(Do not include the title "Other Items" in the ISA.) If the technical representatives determine that any item below is "not applicable," a statement to that effect may be made in the ISA in lieu of eliminating the item from the ISA. For example, if there is no dialup connectivity, the appropriate entry would be "Dialup capability will not be used by either interconnected system."*

+ *Security Parameters.* Specify the security parameters exchanged between systems to authenticate that the requesting system is the legitimate system and that the class(es) of service requested is approved by the ISA. For example, at the system level, if a new service such as e-mail is requested without prior coordination, it should be detected, refused, and documented as a possible intrusion until the interconnected service is authorized. Also, additional security parameters may be required (e.g., personal accountability) to allow the respondent system to determine whether a requestor is authorized to receive the information and/or services requested and whether all details of the transaction fall within the scope of user services authorized in the ISA.

+ *Operational Security Mode.* If both parties use the concept of Protection Levels and Levels-of-Concern for Confidentiality, Integrity, and Availability based on their implementation common

---

[8] The organizations may choose to address other relevant items in the ISA, in addition to the suggested items.

criteria, enter the values for each as documented for both systems. Optionally, the security mode of operations could be documented for both systems.

+ *Training and Awareness.* Enter the details of any new or additional security training and awareness requirements, and the assignment of responsibility for conducting training and awareness throughout the life cycle of the interconnection.

+ *Specific Equipment Restrictions.* Describe any revised or new restriction(s) to be placed on terminals, including their usage, location, and physical accessibility.

+ *Dialup and Broadband Connectivity.* Describe any special considerations for dialup and broadband connections to any system in the proposed interconnection, including security risks and safeguards used to mitigate those risks. See National Institute of Standards and Technology (NIST) Special Publication 800-46, *Security Guide for Telecommuting and Broadband Communications*, for more information.

+ *Security Documentation.* Enter the title and general details of each organization's system security plan, including the assignment of responsibilities for developing and accepting the plan, as well as any other relevant documentation.

A.8   Section 3: Topological Drawing

The ISA should include a topological drawing illustrating the interconnectivity from one system to the other system (end-point to end-point). The drawing should include the following:

+ The title "SECTION 3: TOPOLOGICAL DRAWING."

+ All communications paths, circuits, and other components used for the interconnection, from "Organization A's" system to "Organization B's" system.

+ The drawing should depict the logical location of all components (e.g., firewalls, routers, switches, hubs, servers, encryption devices, and computer workstations).

+ If required, mark the top and bottom of each page with an appropriate handling requirement, such as "FOR OFFICIAL USE ONLY" or "FOR INTERNAL USE ONLY."

A.9   Section 4: Signatory Authority

The ISA should include a signature line. Optionally, this section may include any statements that the two DAAs desire in order to finalize the ISA. This section should include the following:

+ The expiration date of the agreement

+ Periodic review requirements, such as the date of the next review

+ Other statements as required by the DAAs, if any

+ The signatures of the DAAs from each organization, and the date of the signatures.

FOR OFFICIAL USE ONLY

INTERCONNECTION SECURITY AGREEMENT

Between "Organization A"
and
"Organization B"

(ORGANIZATIONAL SEAL[S] HERE)

(DATE HERE)

(Organization A)   (Organization B)

FOR OFFICIAL USE ONLY

Figure A-1. ISA Sample

INTERCONNECTION SECURITY AGREEMENT

SECTION 1: INTERCONNECTION STATEMENT OF REQUIREMENTS

The requirements for interconnection between "Organization A" and "Organization B" are for the express purpose of exchanging data between "System A," owned by Organization A, and "System B," owned by Organization B. Organization B requires the use of Organization A's "XYZ database" and Organization A requires the use of Organization B's "ABC database," as approved and directed by the Secretary of "Agency" in "Proclamation A," dated (date). The expected benefit is to expedite the processing of data associated with "Project R" within prescribed timelines.

SECTION 2: SYSTEM SECURITY CONSIDERATIONS

- **General Information/Data Description.** The interconnection between System A, owned by Organization A, and System B, owned by Organization B, is a two-way path. The purpose of the interconnection is to deliver the XYZ database to Organization B's Data Analysis Department and to deliver the ABC database to Organization A's Research Office.

- **Services Offered.** No user services are offered. This connection only exchanges data between Organization A's system and Organization B's system via a dedicated in-house connection.

- **Data Sensitivity.** The sensitivity of data exchanged between Organization A and Organization B is *Sensitive-But-Unclassified*.

- **User Community.** All Organization A users with access to the data received from Organization B are U.S. citizens with a valid and current Organization A background investigation. All Organization B users with access to the data received from Organization A are U.S. citizens with a valid and current Organization B background investigation.

- **Information Exchange Security.** The security of the information being passed on this two-way connection is protected through the use of FIPS 140-2 approved encryption mechanisms. The connections at each end are located within controlled access facilities, guarded 24 hours a day. Individual users will not have access to the data except through their systems security software inherent to the operating system. All access is controlled by authentication methods to validate the approved users.

Figure A-1. Continued

FOR OFFICIAL USE ONLY

- **Trusted Behavior Expectations.** Organization A's system and users are expected to protect Organization B's ABC database, and Organization B's system and users are expected to protect Organization A's XYZ database, in accordance with the Privacy Act and Trade Secrets Act (18 U.S. Code 1905) and the Unauthorized Access Act (18 U.S. Code 2701 and 2710).

- **Formal Security Policy.** Policy documents that govern the protection of the data are Organization A's "XXX Policy" and Organization B's "YYY Policy."

- **Incident Reporting.** The party discovering a security incident will report it in accordance with its incident reporting procedures. In the case of Organization B, any security incident will be reported to the Computer Security Incident Response Capability located at the Data Security Complex. Policy governing the reporting of security incidents is CC-2234.

- **Audit Trail Responsibilities.** Both parties are responsible for auditing application processes and user activities involving the interconnection. Activities that will be recorded include event type, date and time of event, user identification, workstation identification, success or failure of access attempts, and security actions taken by system administrators or security officers. Audit logs will be retained for one (1) year.

SECTION 3: TOPOLOGICAL DRAWING

(Insert a drawing here.)

SECTION 4: SIGNATORY AUTHORITY

This ISA is valid for one (1) year after the last date on either signature below. At that time it will be updated, reviewed, and reauthorized. Either party may terminate this agreement upon 30 days' advanced notice in writing or in the event of a security incident that necessitates an immediate response.

(Organization A Official)   **(Organization B Official)**

_____   _____
(Signature   Date)   (Signature   Date)

FOR OFFICIAL USE ONLY

2

Figure A-1. Continued

Appendix B—Memorandum of Understanding/Agreement

The organizations that own and operate the connected systems should establish a Memorandum of Understanding (or Agreement) (MOU/A) (or an equivalent document) that defines the responsibilities of both parties in establishing, operating, and securing the interconnection. This management document should not contain technical details of the interconnection. Those details should be addressed separately in the Interconnection Security Agreement (ISA) (see Appendix A).

An MOU/A development guide is provided below, although organizations may use their own MOU/A format, if appropriate. Figure B-1 depicts a sample MOU/A.

B.1   Supersession

Identify any previous agreements that this memorandum supersedes, including document titles and dates. If the memorandum does not supersede any other agreements, so state.

B.2   Introduction

Use this section to describe the purpose of the memorandum. Sample language is provided in the sample memorandum. Identify the organizations and IT systems that are involved in the interconnection.

B.3   Authorities

Identify any relevant legislative, regulatory, or policy authorities on which the MOU/A is based.

B.4   Background

Use this section to describe the IT systems that will be connected; the data that will be shared, exchanged, or passed one-way across the interconnection; and the business purpose for the interconnection.

The description of the systems should be brief and nontechnical. The goal is to identify the systems and their boundaries. The memorandum should not provide system specifications. This section should include the formal name of each system; briefly describe their functions; identify their physical locations; identify their sensitivity or classification level; and identify the type(s) of data they store, process, and/or transmit.

B.5   Communications

Discuss the communications that will be exchanged between the parties throughout the duration of the interconnection. Identify the specific events for which the parties must exchange formal notification, and discuss the nature of such communications.

B.6   Interconnecting Security Agreement

State that the parties will jointly develop and sign an ISA before the systems can be connected. In addition, describe the purpose of the ISA.

B.7 Security

State that both parties agree to abide by the security arrangements specified in the ISA. In addition, state that both parties certify that their respective system is designed, managed, and operated in compliance with all relevant federal laws, regulations, and policies.

B.8 Cost Considerations

This section provides the financial details of the agreement. It specifies who will pay for each part of the interconnection and the conditions under which financial commitments may be made. Typically, each organization is responsible for the equipment necessary to interconnect its local system, whereas the organizations jointly fund the interconnecting mechanism or media. However, the financial arrangements are fully negotiable.

B.9 Timeline

Identify the expiration date of the memorandum and procedures for reauthorizing it. In addition, stipulate that the memorandum may be terminated with written notice from one of the parties to the other. The memorandum and the ISA should have the same expiration date.

B.10 Signatory Authority

The memorandum must include a signature line, containing two signature blocks for each designated approval authority. Place the two signature blocks on the same line: one signature on the left and one on the right. Include an area for the "date" signed.

FOR OFFICIAL USE ONLY

MEMORANDUM OF UNDERSTANDING (OR AGREEMENT)

Between "Organization A"
and
"Organization B"

(ORGANIZATIONAL SEAL[S] HERE)

(DATE HERE)

(Organization A)   (Organization B)

FOR OFFICIAL USE ONLY

Figure B-1. MOU/A Sample

FOR OFFICIAL USE ONLY

MEMORANDUM OF UNDERSTANDING (OR AGREEMENT)

SUPERSEDES: (None or document title and date)

INTRODUCTION

The purpose of this memorandum is to establish a management agreement between "Organization A" and "Organization B" regarding the development, management, operation, and security of a connection between "System A," owned by Organization A, and "System B," owned by Organization B.   This agreement will govern the relationship between Organization A and Organization B, including designated managerial and technical staff, in the absence of a common management authority.

AUTHORITY

The authority for this agreement is based on "Proclamation A" issued by the Secretary of the "Agency" on (date).

BACKGROUND

It is the intent of both parties to this agreement to interconnect the following information technology (IT) systems to exchange data between "ABC database" and "XYZ database." Organization A requires the use of Organization B's ABC database, and Organization B requires the use of Organization A's XYZ database, as approved and directed by the Secretary of Agency in Proclamation A. The expected benefit of the interconnection is to expedite the processing of data associated with "Project R" within prescribed timelines.

Each IT system is described below:

- **SYSTEM A**
    - Name
    - Function
    - Location
    - Description of data, including sensitivity or classification level

- **SYSTEM B**
    - Name
    - Function
    - Location
    - Description of data, including sensitivity or classification level

FOR OFFICIAL USE ONLY

1

Figure B-1. Continued

COMMUNICATIONS

Frequent formal communications are essential to ensure the successful management and operation of the interconnection. The parties agree to maintain open lines of communication between designated staff at both the managerial and technical levels. All communications described herein must be conducted in writing unless otherwise noted.

The owners of System A and System B agree to designate and provide contact information for technical leads for their respective system, and to facilitate direct contacts between technical leads to support the management and operation of the interconnection. To safeguard the confidentiality, integrity, and availability of the connected systems and the data they store, process, and transmit, the parties agree to provide notice of specific events within the time frames indicated below:

- **Security Incidents:** Technical staff will immediately notify their designated counterparts by telephone or e-mail when a security incident(s) is detected, so the other party may take steps to determine whether its system has been compromised and to take appropriate security precautions. The system owner will receive formal notification in writing within five (5) business days after detection of the incident(s).

- **Disasters and Other Contingencies:** Technical staff will immediately notify their designated counterparts by telephone or e-mail in the event of a disaster or other contingency that disrupts the normal operation of one or both of the connected systems.

- **Material Changes to System Configuration:** Planned technical changes to the system architecture will be reported to technical staff before such changes are implemented. The initiating party agrees to conduct a risk assessment based on the new system architecture and to modify and re-sign the ISA within one (1) month of implementation.

- **New Interconnections:** The initiating party will notify the other party at least one (1) month *before* it connects its IT system with any other IT system, including systems that are owned and operated by third parties.

- **Personnel Changes:** The parties agree to provide notification of the separation or long-term absence of their respective system owner or technical lead. In addition, both parties will provide notification of any changes in point of contact information. Both parties also will provide notification of changes to user profiles, including users who resign or change job responsibilities.

2

Figure B-1. Continued

FOR OFFICIAL USE ONLY

INTERCONNECTION SECURITY AGREEMENT

The technical details of the interconnection will be documented in an Interconnection Security Agreement (ISA). The parties agree to work together to develop the ISA, which must be signed by both parties before the interconnection is activated. Proposed changes to either system or the interconnecting medium will be reviewed and evaluated to determine the potential impact on the interconnection. The ISA will be renegotiated before changes are implemented. Signatories to the ISA shall be the DAA for each system.

SECURITY

Both parties agree to work together to ensure the joint security of the connected systems and the data they store, process, and transmit, as specified in the ISA. Each party certifies that its respective system is designed, managed, and operated in compliance with all relevant federal laws, regulations, and policies.

COST CONSIDERATIONS

Both parties agree to equally share the costs of the interconnecting mechanism and/or media, but no such expenditures or financial commitments shall be made without the written concurrence of both parties. Modifications to either system that are necessary to support the interconnection are the responsibility of the respective system owners' organization.

TIMELINE

This agreement will remain in effect for one (1) year after the last date on either signature in the signature block below. After one (1) year, this agreement will expire without further action. If the parties wish to extend this agreement, they may do so by reviewing, updating, and reauthorizing this agreement. The newly signed agreement should explicitly supersede this agreement, which should be referenced by title and date. If one or both of the parties wish to terminate this agreement prematurely, they may do so upon 30 days' advanced notice or in the event of a security incident that necessitates an immediate response.

SIGNATORY AUTHORITY

I agree to the terms of this Memorandum of Understanding (or Agreement).

(Organization A Official)   **(Organization B Official)**

_____   _____
(Signature   Date)   (Signature   Date)

FOR OFFICIAL USE ONLY

3

Figure B-1 – Continued.

B-6

Appendix C—System Interconnection Implementation Plan

Appendix C provides guidance for developing a System Interconnection Implementation Plan and is based on the discussion in Section 4. In addition, refer to NIST Special Publication 800-27, *Engineering Principles for Information Technology Security (A Baseline for Achieving Security),* for guidance on security principles that should be incorporated into planning activities.

C.1   Introduction

Describe the purpose and scope of the implementation plan, and identify policy requirements or guidance on which the system interconnection is based. Identify the information technology (IT) systems that will be interconnected, the organizations that own them, and the purpose for which they are used. Discuss the purpose for interconnecting the systems, and describe the services that will be offered over the interconnection. Briefly describe each section of the document.

C.2   System Interconnection Description

Describe the architecture of the interconnection, including security controls, hardware, software, servers, and applications. Provide a diagram of the interconnection, showing all relevant components.

C.2.1   Security Controls

Identify and describe the security controls that are currently in place for the IT systems that will be interconnected. Identify the threats that could compromise the system interconnection and describe how existing security controls will be configured to mitigate those threats. Identify any new security controls that will be implemented, including network- and application-level controls.

C.2.2   System Hardware

Hardware is the physical equipment associated with an IT system. Identify and describe the hardware that is currently used on the systems that will be interconnected, and describe how it will support the interconnection. Identify and describe any new hardware that will be installed as part of the interconnection, including its function.

C.2.3   System Software

Software includes the application programs, software routines, and operating system software associated with an IT system. Identify and describe software currently used on the systems that will be interconnected, and describe how it will be used to support the interconnection. Identify any new software that will be installed as part of the interconnection, including its function.

C.2.4   Data/Information Exchange

Organizations connect IT systems to share data, make data available, or pass data one-way from one organization to the other. It may be necessary to install a database that is dedicated to the interconnection. Identify the type(s) of data that will be exchanged between the organizations, and describe the transmission methods that will be used. Identify how the data will be stored and processed. Provide a data flow diagram.

C.2.5 Services and Applications

Describe the services and applications that the participating organizations will provide over the interconnection, as well as any new services or applications that will be developed, both initially and in the future. Examples include e-mail, database query, file query, and general computational services, application servers, and authentication servers.

C.3 Roles and Responsibilities

Identify the personnel who will establish and maintain the system interconnection, and define their respective roles and responsibilities. A variety of staff skills may be required, including a program manager, network architect, security specialist, system administrator, network administrator, database administrator, application developer, and graphics designer. Staff from both organizations should be involved, if appropriate. Also, identify the responsibilities of staff who will be authorized to use the interconnection after it is established (i.e., the users). The interconnection rules of behavior should be consulted when developing this section.

C.4 Tasks and Procedures

Provide a step-by-step approach to establishing the interconnection, based on a series of tasks and procedures. A list of suggested tasks is provided below. Organizations should view them in the context of their own requirements. In addition, provide a checklist for each task to ensure it is performed properly.

C.4.1 Implement Security Controls

The process of interconnecting IT systems could open an organization to a range of security vulnerabilities. Consequently, the first step that organizations should take is to implement appropriate security controls. Provide procedures for configuring current controls and, if necessary, implementing new controls. Security controls may include firewalls, identification and authentication mechanisms, logical access controls, encryption devices, intrusion detection systems (IDS), and physical security measures.

C.4.2 Install Hardware and Software

Provide procedures for configuring or installing hardware and software to establish the interconnection, if required.

C.4.3 Integrate Applications

Provide procedures for linking applications across the interconnection, if required. Also, provide procedures for developing and implementing new applications, if required.

C.4.4 Conduct a Risk Assessment[9]

Describe the process for conducting an assessment to identify risks associated with the newly established interconnection, or refer to an organization's existing risk assessment methodology. Discuss how risks will be addressed. For example, risks may be mitigated by adjusting security controls or by implementing additional countermeasures.

---

[9] Alternately, each organization may decide to recertify and reaccredit its respective system, as discussed in Section 4.2.7.

C.4.5 Conduct Operational and Security Testing

Provide detailed test procedures to verify whether the interconnection operates efficiently and securely. Also, describe how the results of the testing will be measured, and how deficiencies will be addressed.

C.4.6 Conduct Security Training and Awareness

Describe a training and awareness program for all personnel who will be authorized to manage, use, and/or operate the system interconnection, including any new computer applications associated with it. Training should ensure that authorized personnel know the rules of behavior associated with the interconnection and how to request assistance if they encounter problems. In addition, personnel who are responsible for maintaining the interconnection should receive specialized training to ensure they are proficient in their responsibilities.

C.5 Schedule And Budget

Provide a schedule for establishing the interconnection, including the estimated time required to complete each task. Also, define a budget for the project, and describe how costs will be apportioned between the participating organizations, if required.

C.6 Documentation

Cite or include all documentation that is relevant for establishing the interconnection, including system security plans, design specifications, and standard operating procedures.

Appendix D—Glossary

Selected terms used in the *Security Guide for Interconnecting Information Technology Systems* are defined below.

Access Control: The process of granting access to information technology (IT) system resources only to authorized users, programs, processes, or other systems.

Audit Trail: A record showing who has accessed an IT system and what operations the user has performed during a given period.

Authentication: The process of verifying the authorization of a user, process, or device, usually as a prerequisite for granting access to resources in an IT system.

Certification and Accreditation (C&A): Certification involves the testing and evaluation of the technical and nontechnical security features of an IT system to determine its compliance with a set of specified security requirements. Accreditation is a process whereby a Designated Approval Authority (DAA) or other authorizing management official authorizes an IT system to operate for a specific purpose using a defined set of safeguards at an acceptable level of risk.

Data Element: A basic unit of information that has a unique meaning and subcategories (data items) of distinct value. Examples of data elements include gender, race, and geographic location.

Dedicated Line: A leased or privately owned transmission line that provides a constant transmission path from point A to point B.

Disconnection: The termination of an interconnection between two or more IT systems. A disconnection may be planned (e.g., due to changed business needs) or unplanned (i.e., due to an attack or other contingency).

Encryption: The translation of data into a form that is unintelligible without a deciphering mechanism.

File Transfer Protocol (FTP): A service that supports file transfer between local and remote computers.

Firewall: A system designed to prevent unauthorized access to or from a private network. Firewalls can be implemented in both hardware and software, or a combination of both.

Hub: A common connection point for devices in a network. Hubs commonly are used to pass data from one device (or segment) to another.

Identification: The process of verifying the identity of a user, process, or device, usually as a prerequisite for granting access to resources in an IT system.

Integrated Services Digital Network (ISDN): A public-switched network providing digital connections for the concurrent transmission of voice, video, data, and images.

Interconnection Security Agreement (ISA): In this guide, an agreement established between the organizations that own and operate connected IT systems to document the technical requirements of the interconnection. The ISA also supports a Memorandum of Understanding or Agreement (MOU/A) between the organizations.

Intrusion Detection System (IDS): A software application that can be implemented on host operating systems or as network devices to monitor activity that is associated with intrusions or insider misuse, or both.

Java: A programming language developed by Sun Microsystems. Java contains a number of features that make it well suited for use on the World Wide Web.

JavaScript: A scripting language for use in developing interactive Web sites.

Kerberos: An authentication system developed at the Massachusetts Institute of Technology (MIT). Kerberos is designed to enable two parties to exchange private information across a public network.

Memorandum of Understanding/Agreement (MOU/A): A document established between two or more parties to define their respective responsibilities in accomplishing a particular goal or mission. In this guide, an MOU/A defines the responsibilities of two or more organizations in establishing, operating, and securing a system interconnection.

RADIUS (Remote Authentication Dial-In User Service): An authentication and accounting system used to control access to an Internet Service Provider (ISP) system.

Risk: The net mission impact considering the probability that a particular threat will exercise (accidentally trigger or intentionally exploit) a particular information system vulnerability and the resulting impact if this should occur.

Router: On a network, a device that determines the best path for forwarding a data packet toward its destination. The router is connected to at least two networks, and is located at the gateway where one network meets another.

Security Controls: Protective measures used to meet the security requirements specified for IT resources.

Server: A computer or device on a network that manages network resources. Examples include file servers (to store files), print servers (to manage one or more printers), network servers (to manage network traffic), and database servers (to process database queries).

Switch: A network device that filters and forwards packets between LAN segments.

System Interconnection: The direct connection of two or more IT systems for the purpose of sharing data and other information resources.

T1 Line: A telecommunications line with bandwidth capacity of 1.54 Mbps.

T3 Line: A telecommunications line with bandwidth capacity of 45 Mbps.

Threat: The potential for a threat-source to exercise (accidentally trigger or intentionally exploit) a specific vulnerability.

Trojan Horse: A computer program containing an apparent or actual useful function that also contains additional functions that permit the unauthorized collection, falsification, or destruction of data.

Virtual Private Network (VPN): A data network that enables two or more parties to communicate securely across a public network by creating a private connection, or "tunnel," between them.

Virus: A computer program containing a malicious segment that attaches itself to an application program or other executable component.

Vulnerability: A flaw or weakness in system security procedures, design, implementation, or internal controls that could be exercised (accidentally triggered or intentionally exploited) and result in a security breach or a violation of the system's security policy.

Worm: A computer program or algorithm that replicates itself over a computer network and usually performs malicious actions.

Appendix E—References

Christopher King. "Extranet Access Control Issues," in Harold F. Tipton and Micki Krause, ed., *Information Security Management Handbook.* Vol. 2, 4th ed., New York: Auerbach, 2000, pp. 99-114.

Defense Authorization Act (Fiscal Year 2001). Public Law 106-398, Title X, Subtitle G. *Government Information Security Reform.* October 30, 2000.

Department of Health and Human Services. *Automated Information Systems Security Program Handbook.* http://irm.cit.nih.gov/policy/aissp.html

"Federal Reserve: Sound Practices Guidance on Information Security." *Computer Security Journal,* Vol. XIV, No.1, 1998, pp. 45-68.

Herold, Rebecca and Slemo Warigon. "Extranet Audit and Security." *Computer Security Journal*, Vol. XIV, No. 1, 1998, pp. 35-44.

GartnerGroup. "Extranet Security: Five Ways to Manage High-Stakes Risk." Research Note, July 21, 1997.

GartnerGroup. "Securing the Extranet: A Statement of Understanding." Research Note, January 20, 1998.

National Institute of Standards and Technology. Federal Information Processing Standards (FIPS) 186-2, *Digital Signature Standard (DSS).* January 2000.

National Institute of Standards and Technology. Special Publication 800-3, *Establishing a Computer Security Incidence Response Capability (CSIRC).* November 1991.

National Institute of Standards and Technology. Special Publication 800-9, *Good Security Practices for Electronic Commerce, Including Electronic Data Interchange.* December 1993.

National Institute of Standards and Technology. Special Publication 800-12, *An Introduction to Computer Security: The NIST Handbook.* October 1995.

National Institute of Standards and Technology. Special Publication 800-14, *Generally Accepted Principles and Practices for Securing Information Technology Systems.* September 1996.

National Institute of Standards and Technology. Special Publication 800-18, *Guide for Developing Security Plans for Information Technology Systems.* December 1998.

National Institute of Standards and Technology. Special Publication 800-26, *Security Self-Assessment Guide for Information Technology Systems.* November 2001.

National Institute of Standards and Technology. Special Publication 800-27, *Engineering Principles for Information Technology Security (A Baseline for Achieving Security).* June 2001.

National Institute of Standards and Technology. Special Publication 800-28, *Guidelines on Active Content and Mobile Code.* October 2001.

National Institute of Standards and Technology. Special Publication 800-30, *Risk Management Guide for Information Technology Systems*. January 2002.

National Institute of Standards and Technology. Special Publication 800-31, *Intrusion Detection Systems (IDS)*. November 2001.

National Institute of Standards and Technology. Special Publication 800-33, *Underlying Technical Models for Information Technology Security*. December 2001.

National Institute of Standards and Technology. Special Publication 800-34, *Contingency Planning Guide for Information Technology Systems*. June 2002.

National Institute of Standards and Technology. Special Publication 800-41, *Guidelines on Firewalls and Firewall Policy*. January 2002.

National Institute of Standards and Technology. Special Publication 800-42, *Guidelines on Network Security Testing*. Forthcoming.

National Institute of Standards and Technology. Special Publication 800-46, *Security Guide for Telecommuting and Broadband Communications*. August 2002.

National Institute of Standards and Technology. Special Publication 800-50, *Building an Information Technology Security Awareness and Training Program*. Forthcoming.

Norman E. Smith. "The Next Great Networking Frontier." September 27, 1999. http://webdeveloper.earthweb.com/webecom/article/0,,11985_616141,00.html

Office of Management and Budget (OMB). Circular A-130, *Management of Federal Information Resources, Security of Federal Automated Information Resources, Appendix III*. November 2000.

Online Source. "Establishing an Extranet: Overview." www.office.com/global

Public Law 100-235. *Computer Security Act of 1987*. January 8, 1988.

Solutionary. "How to Protect Information: A Comprehensive Guide to Securing Networks and Systems." 2001. www.solutionary.com

U.S. Customs Service. "Interconnection Security Agreements." August 25, 2000. www.bsp.gsa.gov/list.cfm

Appendix F—Index